The Little Book of

Happiness

Felicity Forster

SIRIUS

This edition published in 2025 by Sirius Publishing, a division of
Arcturus Publishing Limited,
26/27 Bickels Yard, 151–153 Bermondsey Street,
London SE1 3HA

Copyright © Arcturus Holdings Limited

All rights reserved. No part of this publication may be reproduced, stored
in a retrieval system, or transmitted, in any form or by any means,
electronic, mechanical, photocopying, recording or otherwise, without
prior written permission in accordance with the provisions of the
Copyright Act 1956 (as amended). Any person or persons who do any
unauthorised act in relation to this publication may be liable to criminal
prosecution and civil claims for damages.

ISBN: 978-1-3988-5773-5
AD012759NT

Printed in China

INTRODUCTION

Happiness is good for us – it energizes us, increases our satisfaction with life, strengthens our emotional resources and even improves our physical health. When we're happy, we sleep better, think better, have more energy, communicate better and even live longer.

Happy people like their jobs, find joy and fulfilment in their relationships, enjoy working towards their goals and live in harmony with their morals and values. They may or may not have material wealth, but more often than not they enjoy simple pleasures such as reading a book, drinking a cup of tea, stroking a pet or pottering around the garden.

There's often a misconception that we'll find happiness only after certain milestones are reached – when we get our dream job, find the right partner, buy a house, have children, make enough money – but the truth is these things are no guarantee of happiness. On the contrary, living in the present moment and finding joy in the ordinary pleasures of everyday life is a much better road to happiness. There are plenty of strategies that we can put in place to navigate this road, such as developing our friendships, trying new and challenging activities and finding purpose in our lives. It's not the destination but the journey that counts.

This little book of happiness is full of inspirational quotes and step-by-step exercises that will give you some tools for finding happiness. Dip in whenever you need a pick-me-up, and you may discover that the old saying can sometimes be true: if life is giving you lemons, it's time to start making lemonade!

'The greater part of our happiness or misery depends upon our dispositions, and not upon our circumstances.'

Martha Washington

'They say a person needs just three things to be truly happy in this world: someone to love, something to do, and something to hope for.'

Tom Bodett

Write a thank you letter

Expressing gratitude makes us feel better, and it can be powerful to put such thoughts into writing, especially if you've never properly thanked that person before.

❶ Sit quietly and think of someone who has helped you or done something that changed your life for the better – maybe a teacher or mentor.

❷ Make some notes about how they helped you. What did they say or do? How did this make you feel?

❸ Write a detailed letter of thanks to that person.

❹ If the person is still alive, you might send the letter to them. If not, you'll find that the mere act of expressing your thanks is helpful.

'Happiness cannot be traveled to, owned, earned, worn or consumed. Happiness is the spiritual experience of living every minute with love, grace, and gratitude.'

Denis Waitley

'Being happy never goes out of style.'

Lily Pulitzer

'Let no one ever come to you without leaving better and happier. Be the living expression of God's kindness: kindness in your face, kindness in your eyes, kindness in your smile.'

Mother Teresa

Notice
the everyday

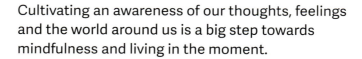

Cultivating an awareness of our thoughts, feelings and the world around us is a big step towards mindfulness and living in the moment.

❶ Go for a walk and make a conscious effort to notice the air moving past you, the temperature of the air and whether there's any wind blowing or rain falling.

❷ Pay attention to everything your senses are telling you. What can you see? What can you smell? Are there any sounds? How do your feet feel on the ground?

❸ Next time you have a meal, make an effort to really savour the food and drink. Notice the tastes, textures and aromas, and take your time to enjoy all those sensations.

'Everyone wants to live on top of the mountain, but all the happiness and growth occurs while you're climbing it.'

Andy Rooney

'You will never be happy if you continue to search for what happiness consists of. You will never live if you are looking for the meaning of life.'

Albert Camus

'The most wasted
of days is one
without laughter.'

e e cummings

Meditate and
elevate

Regular meditation can elevate your mood and give you feelings of quiet contentment. If you do it successfully, it will make you feel less stressed and give you more energy.

❶ Find a quiet place where you won't be disturbed.

❷ Sit with your back straight and relax your neck and shoulders.

❸ Inhale through your nose, and as you do so, count slowly to 4.

❹ Hold your breath and count to 7.

❺ Exhale through your mouth and count to 8.

'Happiness is amazing. It's so amazing it doesn't matter if it's yours or not.'

Ricky Gervais

'For every minute you are angry you lose sixty seconds of happiness.'

Ralph Waldo Emerson

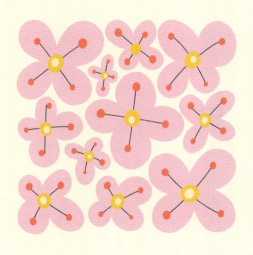

Laugh

As the old saying goes, laughter is the best medicine. It's also been said that if you can laugh in the face of adversity, you're bulletproof. Laughter brings people together, releases endorphins, boosts our immune system and relaxes our whole body. Seeking out opportunities for humour and laughter could even make us live longer.

❶ Look for ways of bringing humour into everyday conversations. Ask a friend, 'What's the funniest thing that's ever happened to you?'

❷ Spend time with people who laugh easily and who make you laugh. Schedule fun activities to do together, such as playing games or sports.

❸ Watch a comedy movie or read a humorous book.

❹ Go to a live comedy show. Laughter becomes surprisingly contagious when you're part of an audience.

'Happiness is not the absence of problems, it's the ability to deal with them.'

Steve Maraboli

'I'd far rather be happy than right any day.'

Douglas Adams

'So we shall let the reader answer this question for himself: who is the happier man, he who has braved the storm of life and lived or he who has stayed securely on shore and merely existed?'

Hunter S. Thompson

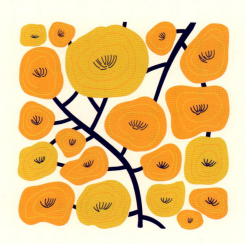

Get into
the groove

Music can have a hugely positive impact on our health and emotions, giving us feelings of happiness and wellbeing, helping us to overcome sadness and stimulating happy memories of our youth. When we listen to music, our feel-good hormone dopamine is released, activating our brain's pleasure and reward system. Try making some playlists of your favourite songs or pieces of classical music, ready to play on different occasions or to create particular moods.

❶ If you're getting ready to go out socialising, choose upbeat, energetic music that will get you dancing.

❷ For studying, classical music is good for background atmosphere. It can keep your brain active but not interrupt your flow of thoughts.

❸ When you want to relax at the end of the day, choose calming, meditative music that will lower your heart rate and deepen your breathing.

'I felt once more how simple and frugal a thing is happiness: a glass of wine, a roast chestnut, a wretched little brazier, the sound of the sea. Nothing else.'

Nikos Kazantzakis

'One of the keys to happiness is a bad memory.'

Rita Mae Brown

'Folks are usually about as happy as they make their minds up to be.'

Abraham Lincoln

Boost your
self-esteem

Having confidence and self-worth is very important in maintaining positive mental health and wellbeing. When you value yourself and feel good about yourself, you are more likely to feel energized and motivated.

❶ Treat yourself as a valued friend.

❷ Pay attention to any negative thoughts you may have, such as 'You were hopeless at yesterday's meeting' and ask yourself, 'Would I talk like that to my best friend?'

❸ Replace your negative thoughts with positive ones, such as 'You're intelligent and you know what you're doing. You'll do much better next time.'

'Happiness depends upon ourselves.'

Aristotle

'It's like Tolstoy said. Happiness is an allegory, unhappiness a *story*.'

Haruki Murakami

'I must learn to be content with being happier than I deserve.'

Jane Austen

Sleep your troubles away

We all need good-quality sleep to feel happy and healthy. When we're asleep, our brain rests and simultaneously processes the events and emotions of the day. Around 7–8 hours is the average time an adult needs to sleep each night.

❶ Clear your mind of distractions and worries by writing a 'to do' list for the next day before bedtime.

❷ Create a healthy routine by going to bed at the same time every evening.

❸ Make sure your bedroom is dark, quiet, cool and free from distractions. Turn off all your electronic devices an hour before bed.

❹ Read a book for a while before turning out the light.

❺ Relax and visualize a calm place, such as a beach, waterfall or wildflower meadow.

'I felt my lungs inflate with the onrush of scenery – air, mountains, trees, people. I thought, "This is what it is to be happy."'

Sylvia Plath

'True happiness is to enjoy the present, without anxious dependence upon the future, not to amuse ourselves with either hopes or fears but to rest satisfied with what we have, which is sufficient, for he that is so wants nothing. The greatest blessings of mankind are within us and within our reach. A wise man is content with his lot, whatever it may be, without wishing for what he has not.'

Seneca

Take
time out

If you ever feel overwhelmed with problems or worries, set aside 10 minutes and sit in a quiet place with no distractions. It may help to write things down or record yourself speaking. Take yourself through the following steps:

❶ What are the problems you are facing?

❷ How have you dealt with similar issues in the past?

❸ What can you do that will help the situation?

❹ Can you look at the situation in a different way? It may be helpful to ask yourself how you'll feel about whatever's upsetting you in a week, a month or a year.

❺ If you need to take action, make a plan and then immediately shift your focus away from the problem.

❻ Carry out your plan when the time is right.

'It was only a sunny smile, and little it cost in the giving, but like morning light it scattered the night and made the day worth living.'

F. Scott Fitzgerald

'Nothing shakes the
smiling heart.'

Santosh Kalwar

'If more of us valued food and cheer and song above hoarded gold, it would be a merrier world.'

J.R.R. Tolkien

Build your resilience

Resilience allows us to deal with life's difficulties as well as helping us to bounce back from setbacks. The more resilient we are, the better we are at getting through tough times.

❶ Begin by thinking about what you're good at, no matter how small. Perhaps you're a good listener or an avid reader.

❷ Now think about areas where you have felt challenged. How did you overcome those difficulties? Try to apply the above skills to these challenges.

❸ Find a metaphor to help you in difficult times. For example, if you have to complete a complicated task, imagine that a DJ has suddenly switched on an upbeat song that gives you a surge of energy.

❹ Reward yourself when you make positive progress – go for a relaxing walk, cook your favourite dish, listen to music or watch a good movie. Over time, you'll find that you're becoming more resilient.

'The happiness of your life depends upon the quality of your thoughts.'

Marcus Aurelius

'Action may not always bring happiness, but there is no happiness without action.'

William James

'Happiness [is] only real when shared.'

Jon Krakauer

Talk and share

Human beings are social by nature, and talking is often helpful in releasing tension and solving problems. Sweeping our worries under the carpet is never a good idea, so keep channels of communication open and talk to a friend, partner, sibling or counsellor whenever you need to. A problem shared is a problem halved.

❶ Cultivate a support network of colleagues and friends in your workplace.

❷ Set aside time to visit or speak to family members regularly.

❸ Say hello to your neighbours and chat to shopkeepers and people you meet while out and about.

❹ Join online groups to meet people with like-minded interests.

❺ Don't hesitate to seek a counsellor any time you want to work through problems or issues.

'Happiness is not a
possession to be prized,
it is a quality of thought,
a state of mind.'

Daphne du Maurier

'With mirth and laughter let old wrinkles come.'

William Shakespeare

'Attitude is a choice. Happiness is a choice. Optimism is a choice. Kindness is a choice. Giving is a choice. Respect is a choice. Whatever choice you make makes you. Choose wisely.'

Roy T. Bennett

Try
something new

Whenever we do something we've never done before, it makes us notice the world in a new and exciting way. New experiences can give us a hit of the feel-good chemical dopamine – and you don't have to bungee jump off a bridge to get it! You can start small.

1. When travelling to work, vary your usual transport – get off the bus earlier and walk part of the way.

2. Sit in a different seat in meetings.

3. Go somewhere new for lunch.

4. Move the furniture around in your home.

5. Cook something you've never tried before.

6. Sign up for a fitness class or online course.

7. Learn a musical instrument or join a choir.

'The secret of happiness is freedom, the secret of freedom is courage.'

Carrie Jones

'All happiness depends on courage and work.'

Honoré de Balzac

Perform acts of
kindness

Our connections to other human beings are hugely important, and helping others not only feels good, it also makes the world a happier place. The more we give, the happier we feel. Here are a few ideas:

❶ Pay someone a compliment.

❷ Say thank you throughout your day – to shopkeepers, bus drivers, strangers, work colleagues, friends and family.

❸ Smile at people who walk past you.

❹ Volunteer to babysit, look after a neighbour's pet or tidy their garden.

❺ Reach out to an old friend and ask how they are.

'Hope

Smiles from the threshold of the year to come,

Whispering "it will be happier"...'

Alfred Lord Tennyson

'Very little is needed to make a happy life; it is all within yourself in your way of thinking.'

Marcus Aurelius

'I'm choosing happiness over suffering, I know I am. I'm making space for the unknown future to fill up my life with yet-to-come surprises.'

Elizabeth Gilbert

Get wet!

It's well known that water makes us happy. Immersing ourselves in warm water lowers our blood pressure and heart rate, quietens our mind, soothes our muscles and helps us to relax. Cold water is also beneficial; taking a cold shower or swimming outdoors activates our sympathetic nervous system, releasing endorphins and improving our response to stress.

❶ Prepare your bathroom with candles, soft music and bath oils and luxuriate in a long, hot bath (or take a hot shower).

❷ Alternatively, try cold water therapy. Gradually reduce the temperature of your normal shower until it's colder than you're used to. If this works for you, try open water swimming as well.

'The best way to cheer yourself is to try to cheer someone else up.'

Mark Twain

'No medicine cures what happiness cannot.'

Gabriel García Márquez

'When the first baby laughed for the first time, its laugh broke into a thousand pieces, and they all went skipping about, and that was the beginning of fairies.'

J.M. Barrie

Enjoy a meal

We all need to eat and drink to survive, but a really special meal is always something to be savoured, anticipated and enjoyed the most.

❶ Preparation is part of the fun. Browse through some cookery books, choose some exciting recipes and go shopping!

❷ Certain mood-boosting foods are known to lift the spirits. These include dark chocolate, bananas, berries, oily fish, nuts and seeds, oats, spinach, avocados, beans, sweet potatoes, chicken and turkey.

❸ Plan ahead for special occasions such as birthdays, Valentine's Day, Easter, Halloween and Christmas, and go to town with your favourite dishes. The finished products will make everyone happy, not to mention giving you a sense of achievement.

'It isn't what you have or who you are or where you are or what you are doing that makes you happy or unhappy. It is what you think about it.'

Dale Carnegie

'Those who are not looking for happiness are the most likely to find it, because those who are searching forget that the surest way to be happy is to seek happiness for others.'

Martin Luther King Jr.

'Happiness is a warm puppy.'

Charles M. Schulz

Do some physical exercise

Keeping active is a great way to be happy. Physical exercise releases chemicals in our brain that lift our mood, and it helps us sleep better, improves our heart health, gives us more energy and lowers our risk of depression.

❶ Find an activity that you enjoy. There are plenty to choose from! Whether you like walking, dancing, jogging, skipping, yoga, swimming, tennis, football, cycling or something else, try as many as you like.

❷ You get the most benefit if you exercise regularly. Aim for at least 30 minutes per day.

❸ To keep you motivated, try exercising with a friend.

'Happiness is an accident of nature, a beautiful and flawless aberration.'

Pat Conroy

'It's been my experience that you can nearly always enjoy things if you make up your mind firmly that you will.'

Lucy Maud Montgomery

Kick your heels up!

Dancing is in our DNA. From birth onwards, we start to sync up the movements of our arms and legs with music. Dance is a fun form of entertainment and exercise, and a great way to release pent-up emotions and express ourselves. Even people who describe themselves as having two left feet can enjoy moving to music. In fact, it's usually quite difficult to remain still when our favourite song comes on.

❶ Play your favourite song and turn up the volume. Dance like no one's watching!

❷ Go online and find a dance workout. There are styles for every taste, age and ability, from 70s disco workouts to hip-hop and jazzercise.

❸ Join a dance class and have lessons. Dancing with a partner makes you part of a team and is a great way to socialise and make new friends.

'There are two ways to get enough. One is to continue to accumulate more and more. The other is to desire less.'

G.K. Chesterton

'Smile more. Smiling can make you and others happy.'

Roy T. Bennett

'I heard a definition once: Happiness is health and a short memory! I wish I'd invented it, because it is very true.'

Audrey Hepburn

Read a good book

As every book lover knows, curling up with a good book can be one of the greatest pleasures of life. We can travel to other lands, experience new emotions and become immersed in other worlds, all from the safety and comfort of our own armchair. Reading has also been shown to induce a relaxing, pleasurable state in our brain, lowering our stress levels and helping us to feel content.

❶ Think about what you're interested in and what you feel like reading. It can help to browse websites and social media sites that make recommendations.

❷ Once you find a favourite author, read other books they've written. Then seek out other books in a similar genre.

❸ Join a book club to find new books and meet like-minded people.

❹ Don't forget audio books. You can enjoy a book just as much while you're travelling to work, walking the dog or doing housework.

'Happiness is having a large, loving, caring, close-knit family in another city.'

George Burns

'The problem with people is they forget that most of the time it's the small things that count.'

Jennifer Niven

'Happiness makes up in height for what it lacks in length.'

Robert Frost

Consider
adopting a pet

Pets give us unconditional love – there's nothing like the joy of coming home to a loyal companion who can't wait to see us and spend time with us. Animals are incredibly good at boosting our mood. They can help us with loneliness and depression, give our lives a sense of purpose and structure, and help children learn about responsibility and improve their social skills.

❶ Do some research about animal shelters and rescue organisations, and ask questions about breeds, behaviour and temperament before deciding which animal to adopt.

❷ Get everything ready before bringing your new companion home. Provide a secure and quiet area with food and water bowls, bedding and toys.

❸ Speak to your vet about the likely cost of veterinary care and think about getting pet insurance for financial peace of mind.

'Let us be grateful to the people who make us happy; they are the charming gardeners who make our souls blossom.'

Marcel Proust

'Now and then it's good to pause in our pursuit of happiness and just be happy.'

Guillaume Apollinaire

'Whoever is happy will make others happy.'

Anne Frank

Cultivate a positive mindset

If you want to be a positive and happy person, it makes logical sense that you need to have more positive thoughts. Positivity is a bit like gardening – if you plant a seed, you need to provide sunlight, water it and look after it, and it will grow. Whatever you feed your thoughts with will flourish.

1. Begin every day with some positive affirmations, such as 'I am excited about what today will bring', 'I deserve love and acceptance' or 'I am strong and capable'.

2. Be grateful for all the good things in your life.

3. Look for the humour in any situation.

4. Practise self-compassion by turning your mistakes into opportunities for learning.

'There is only one way to happiness and that is to cease worrying about things which are beyond the power of our will.'

Epictetus

'"Happily ever after, or even just together ever after, is not cheesy," Wren said. "It's the noblest, like, the most courageous thing two people can shoot for."'

Rainbow Rowell

Stretch!

It feels good to stretch. Stretching activates our parasympathetic nervous system and increases blood flow to our muscles, and generally makes us feel better. After a long day of tension and stress, stretching is one of the quickest and easiest ways to unwind.

1. Cat-cow: To create a cat posture, get down on all fours, round your spine and drop your head down towards the floor. Then do the cow posture by lifting your head, chest and tailbone towards the ceiling and arching your back.

2. Reclined twist: Lie down and hug your knees to your chest. Extend your arms to your sides, then drop both knees gently to one side. Repeat on the other side.

3. Child's pose: Kneel down and slowly bring your torso down over your thighs, bringing your forehead to the floor. Extend your arms in front of you.

'Happiness is holding someone in your arms and knowing you hold the whole world.'

Orhan Pamuk

'People are unhappy when they get something too easily. You have to sweat – that's the only moral they know.'

Dany Laferrière

'We should always make time for the things we like. If we don't, we might forget how to be happy.'

T.J. Klune

Write a gratitude journal

Taking the time to acknowledge the good things in our lives can be helpful in shifting our focus from stress and negativity to calmness and positivity, whether it be noticing the simple joys of nature or recognizing our connections with people.

❶ Choose a journal. You might buy a special notebook or you could use an app on your phone or tablet.

❷ Start by writing down at least three things you feel thankful for in your life. They could be very simple, such as the sound of a bird singing or a smile from a stranger, or a deeper gratitude for the love and understanding you feel from a friend or family member.

❸ Every day, spend a few minutes recording your positive experiences. Writing them down will help you re-experience the positivity all over again.

'I, not events, have the power to make me happy or unhappy today. I can choose which it shall be. Yesterday is dead, tomorrow hasn't arrived yet. I have just one day, today, and I'm going to be happy in it.'

Groucho Marx

'The richness I achieve comes from nature, the source of my inspiration.'

Claude Monet

'Man only likes to count histroubles; he doesn't calculate his happiness.'

Fyodor Dostoevsky

Keep healthy

Health and happiness go together, so making healthy choices in all aspects of our life is a sure way to improve our physical and mental wellbeing.

❶ Eat a healthy, balanced diet that includes all the main food groups. Limit alcohol, which can amplify negative emotions and make you feel depressed.

❷ Establish a healthy bedtime routine and get about 7–8 hours' sleep per night.

❸ Exercise regularly. About 150 minutes a week is recommended.

❹ Avoid overdosing on the news; keep things balanced with more light-hearted entertainment content too.

'Happiness is not a goal . . . it's a by-product of a life well lived.'

Eleanor Roosevelt

'I am not proud, but I am happy;
and happiness blinds, I think,
more than pride.'

Alexandre Dumas

'Cry. Forgive. Learn. Move on. Let your tears water the seeds of your future happiness.'

Steve Maraboli

Accept
what you cannot change

Acknowledging situations as they are rather than continually focusing on how to fix, manage or change them can be a powerful tool in finding happiness. Instead of treating our lives as lists of problems to be solved, acceptance means embracing all our thoughts and emotions instead of avoiding, denying or altering them. It can be surprisingly freeing to accept the things we cannot change.

❶ Accept that lack of control is an unavoidable part of life.

❷ Face problems head-on, then focus on what you can do rather than what you can't.

❸ Let go of the things you cannot change.

❹ Celebrate your accomplishments and be kind to yourself, including when things go wrong.

'Children are happy because they don't have a file in their minds called "All the Things That Could Go Wrong."'

Marianne Williamson

'Success is getting what you want.
Happiness is wanting what you get.'

Dale Carnegie

Follow
your heart

Doing whatever is in tune with your interests and what you feel most passionate about is a watertight recipe for happiness. It can lead to a dream job, a fulfilling friendship, a great partner or a new hobby you'll love so much you'll spend the rest of your life doing it.

❶ Start with some self-reflection. What are your interests? What do you love doing?

❷ What are your strengths? What are you best at?

❸ It can help to think about the happiest moments of your life. What were you doing then? Do these moments have anything in common? If so, they will probably indicate your passions.

❹ Seek ways of following those passions. Put yourself out there!

'You can't be happy unless you're unhappy sometimes.'

Lauren Oliver

'A thing of beauty is a joy forever.'

John Keats

'The power of finding beauty in the humblest things makes home happy and life lovely.'

Louisa May Alcott

Enjoy yourself

Spending time doing things we enjoy is one of the easiest ways to make ourselves happy.

❶ Do more of whatever you enjoy! The list is endless and is different for everyone. It might be cooking, dancing, gardening, having a bath, reading a book, painting, listening to music, meeting friends, walking, watching a movie, swimming, volunteering or playing sport.

❷ Practise self-care. Look after yourself and always make time for relaxation and rest.

'Sanity and happiness are an impossible combination.'

Mark Twain

'The pain I feel now is the happiness I had before. That's the deal.'

C.S. Lewis